BOEING 747

JANE'S

First published in 1984 by Yama-kei Publishers Co Ltd,
Tokyo

Photographs © Hiroshi Seo, 1984

Text © Jane's Publishing Company Limited 1984

First published in the United Kingdom
in 1984 by Jane's Publishing Company Limited
238 City Road, London EC1V 2PU

ISBN 0 7106 0304 5

Distributed in the Philippines and the
USA and its dependencies by
Jane's Publishing Inc
135 West 50th Street
New York, NY 10020

Printed in Japan

Contents

The 747 story

Birth of the 'Jumbo'

The Boeing 747 took to the air in February 1969, some 65 years after the first powered heavier-than-air flight, made by the Wright brothers in December 1903. This time span is less than the average life expectancy of mankind, but in this short time aviation has progressed from that primitive single-pilot biplane which managed to fly just several hundred metres, to giant jet airliners carrying hundreds of passengers across the oceans.

The very first jet-engined airliner built in the USA was the Boeing 707, then a revolutionary giant which carried almost twice as many passengers and cruised twice as fast as previous four-engine aircraft. The spread of such aircraft throughout the world led to the demand for further developments, resulting in the conception of the Boeing 747 project.

The development of passenger aircraft is a sort of gamble. The fact that the present level of technology allows the first examples of a new airliner to be used for test flying, without a prototype in the true sense of the word, underlines the reliability of modern design. Nevertheless, various problems can occur, affecting cost factors and targeted sales:

(Below) In 1954 Boeing completed a prototype aeroplane, the Model 367-80, to compete with the British-built Comet, the world's first production jet airliner. The 707, a scaled-up version of 367-80, began scheduled services in October 1958.

the higher the demand for technological innovation, the greater the risk.

A still bigger question exists on the makers' side. Will a new airliner, developed at enormous cost, be accepted in the market? Obviously, each manufacturer thoroughly surveys the market potential, prepares a forecast of demand, and plans the project to make it attractive to airlines. Yet the objective could be missed, the project deemed unviable and production discontinued. Recent examples are the Concorde supersonic transport and Lockheed L-1011 TriStar.

The 747 project was a risky one indeed. If it should fail, it could cause serious financial damage to Boeing, for apart from the aircraft's unprecedented size - for which the new Pratt & Whitney JT9D engine was yet to be built and proven - a complete plant had to be erected on a new site.

Boeing's project was motivated by the loss to Lockheed of a US Air Force contract for a giant transport aircraft. Considerable investment in manpower and development expenses had to be recouped, while the 707 market had been penetrated by the Douglas DC-8, which

(Above) Lockheed C-5A. Awarded a development contract in September 1965, Lockheed flew the first aeroplane of this type on 30 June 1968. With an overall length of 247 ft 10 in (75.54 m), a width of 228 ft 8.5 in (69.71 m) and a maximum take-off weight of 769 000 lb (348 800 kg), it was the world's biggest aircraft until this accolade passed to the Soviet Antonov An-400.

evolved with a stretched fuselage to cope with a trend towards increased passenger capacity. A larger type of airliner was in demand and Boeing decided to take advantage of the experience gained in designing a giant military transport to pioneer a super-sized civil airliner - the 747.

The design concept of the 747 aimed at reducing the operating cost per passenger by maximizing the load capacity at a cruise speed of Mach 0.92, almost the same as that of previous long-range jet-engined aircraft. Freight capacity was another important consideration, and resulted in the cockpit being located high to ease cargo-loading. This anticipated the possibility of converting the 747 into a freighter rather than a passenger carrier, in view of the US national SST

project, which Boeing was charged to develop in December 1966. This project was a response to the Anglo-French Concorde project, under which a new SST was to be operational by the mid-1970s to fly at a speed of Mach 2.7, with over 220 passengers.

Airlines were of the opinion that the 747 was over-sized, even though the number of air travellers was constantly increasing. However, when Pan American placed an order for 25 aircraft in April 1966, other airlines followed suit to stay in competition. Production was formally decided in July 1966, and the first 747 made its maiden flight on 9 February 1969. Certification was granted on 30 December 1969. Pan Am inaugurated its 747 on the New York-London route on 21 January the following year. Meanwhile, the USA's SST project was dropped, production of Concorde was curtailed and, consequently, the 747 began to play a major role.

The first 747. This historic prototype made its first flight on 9 February 1969, when it flew for 1 hr 16 min. It still serves as Boeing's test aeroplane.

Super-sized aircraft

The 747 was originally proposed as a 'hedge' against the launch of a supersonic transport, but its proposed size surpassed the expectations of many people.

For instance, the Boeing 707 has a floor area of 1143 ft² (106.3 m²) and fuselage width of 148 in (3.76 m). The 747's wide body contains, in its main cabin alone, a floor area of 3529 ft² (328.2 m²), almost three times that of the 707.

With the cabin accommodating up to three times as many passengers as previous jet airliners and its underfloor cargo hold having a load capacity as great as that of an average air freighter, the 747 brought about a considerable reduction in transport costs. Initial calculations estimated that if all the cargo holds were full, the break-even point of 747 would be reached when it was carrying only one third of the passenger load capacity.

As more and more 747s took to the air, competition among airlines intensified, owing to a surplus of air transport capacity. The high capital outlay of a 747 – almost double the cost of a DC-8-61 – presented many airlines with tough investment decisions. However, the 747 started coming into its own as the demand for air travel rose sharply.

Reduced fares for package tours throughout the world contributed to the rapid increase in passenger numbers. Lower group charter fares had already been introduced, but the appearance of the 747 served as the real springboard for the package tour boom.

Air travellers had every reason to welcome the 747, because it greatly enhanced passenger comfort. The cabins are more spacious and the two aisles permit better in-flight services. The quality of in-flight entertainment has improved, and each passenger has access to switches for reading lamps.

Another significant improvement brought about by wide-bodied aircraft, led by the 747, is the noise reduction achieved by high bypass ratio turbofan engines. This is a positive contribution made by the wide-bodies to the sensitive environmental issue of aircraft noise.

(Above left) ANA's Boeing 727-200 has a seating capacity of 178, while its 747SR accommodates 500 passengers. The jumbo's fuselage is about 1.7 times as wide as that of the 727. The cockpit is situated above cabin level, the pilot's seats being 29 ft 0 in (8.84 m) above ground level.

(Above) The Lockheed L-1011 TriStar's fuselage is about 52 ft 6 in (16 m) shorter than that of the 747. For comparison, ANA's L-1011 has 326 passenger seats while JAL's 747SR has 550.

Boeing 747-200 cutaway drawing key

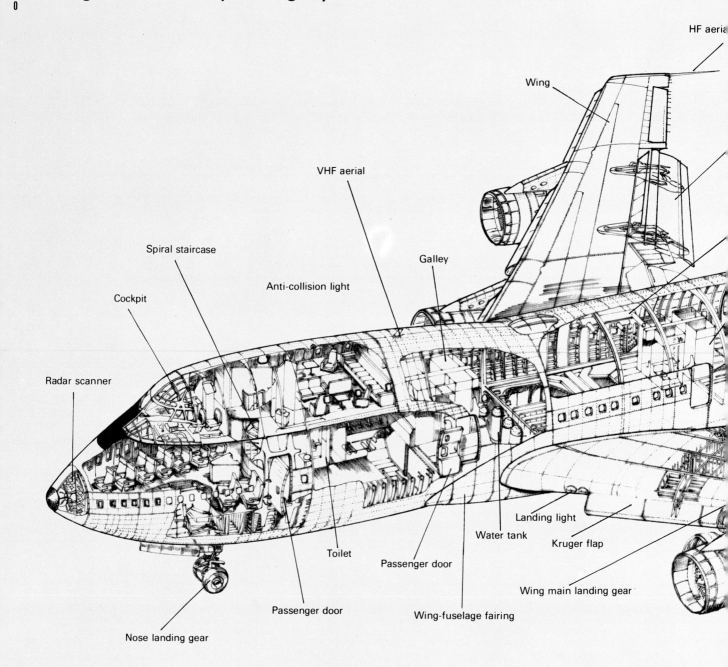

HF aerial

Wing

VHF aerial

Spiral staircase

Galley

Cockpit

Anti-collision light

Radar scanner

Landing light

Water tank

Kruger flap

Toilet

Passenger door

Wing main landing gear

Passenger door

Wing-fuselage fairing

Nose landing gear

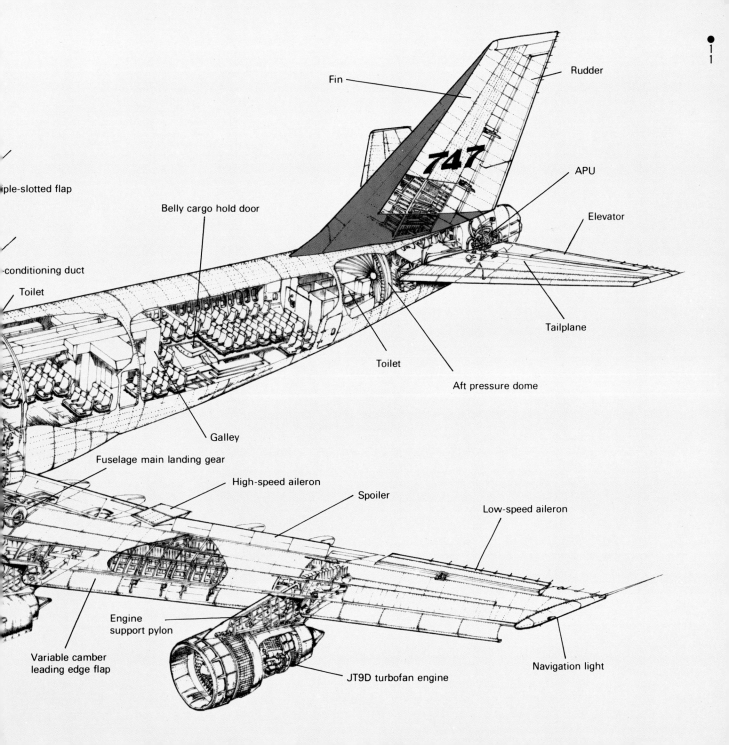

Fin

Rudder

ple-slotted flap

APU

-conditioning duct

Elevator

Belly cargo hold door

Toilet

Tailplane

Toilet

Aft pressure dome

Galley

Fuselage main landing gear

High-speed aileron

Spoiler

Low-speed aileron

Engine
support pylon

Variable camber
leading edge flap

JT9D turbofan engine

Navigation light

747

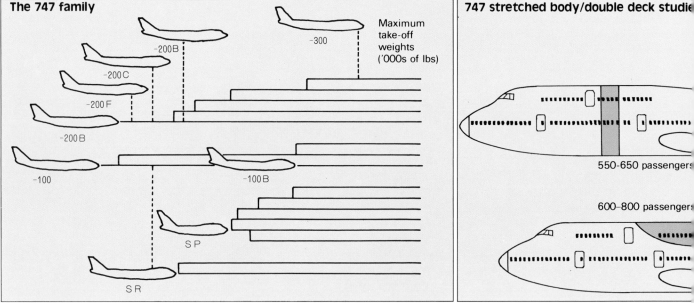

The 747 family

747 stretched body/double deck studie

Maximum take-off weights ('000s of lbs)

-300

-200B

-200C

-200F

-200B

-100

-100B

SP

SR

550-650 passenger

600-800 passenger

The 747 family

The total number of 747s ordered has already passed the 600 mark. All basic airframe dimensions remain the same with the exception of the 747SP, but there are a number of variations.

The earliest version of the 747 was powered by Pratt & Whitney JT9Ds, but from 1974 onwards some models were fitted with the General Electric CF6 and, from 1977, with Rolls-Royce RB.211s.

The first JT9D-3 powerplant had a thrust of 43 500 lb (193 kN), but the latest ones boast an increased thrust of 52 500–54 750 lb (233–243 kN).

A variety of powerplants in terms of type and thrust and a variation of airframe models in terms of maximum take-off gross weight distinguish the many variants of the 747 family. (The difference between the maximum take-off gross weight and the operating empty weight of an aeroplane is equivalent essentially to the load of passengers, cargo, and fuel.)

The first production model 747-100 (flown in February 1969), was powered by JT9Ds and had a maximum take-off weight of 710 000 lb (322 000 kg). It was a little short of capacity to serve on long-range routes. The subsequent series -200B (flown in November 1970) was designed with an increased maximum take-off weight, and became the popular 747 model.

In the -100 series, maximum take-off weight was improved to 735 000 lb (333 400 kg) in the -100A, and to 750 000 lb (340 200 kg) in the -100B in 1979. Another variant is the 747SR (flown in September 1973), which is used only in Japan as a short-range transport. Some -100s have been remodelled into -100SF freighters.

The -200B series reflects further increases in maximum take-off weight, having more powerful engines and increased fuel capacity for long-range flying. Initially, its maximum take-off weight was 775 000 lb (351 500 kg). Now several variants can be selected in this series up to a maximum 833 000 lb (377 850 kg). The -200B Combi has a cargo door on the left rear of the fuselage to allow mixed passenger and freight operation.

As it is a pure freighter variant, the -200F has a nose which hinges upwards for cargo loading and also a rear door to the cargo hold. It was first flown in November 1971. The -200C is another variant with a cargo door and can be converted for passenger or freight service, or can combine the two.

The 747SP, flown in July 1975, has its body length shortened by 48 ft 4 in (14.73 m), a reduced empty operating weight, and improved cruise capability. It is used on extra-long range routes such as Tokyo-New York, which it serves more economically than the 747-200B.

The latest 747 version is the -300, flown in October 1982, which has the upper deck behind the cockpit extended by 23 ft 3 in (7.1 m), thereby increasing the passenger load by about ten per cent.

Stretched-upper-deck 747s on order are limited to passenger models equivalent to the 200B series and to Combi models, but an upper deck extension for the -100B and SR series is also proposed.

For military use, the US Air Force's E-4 command post version and the Iranian Air Force's tanker/freighter are

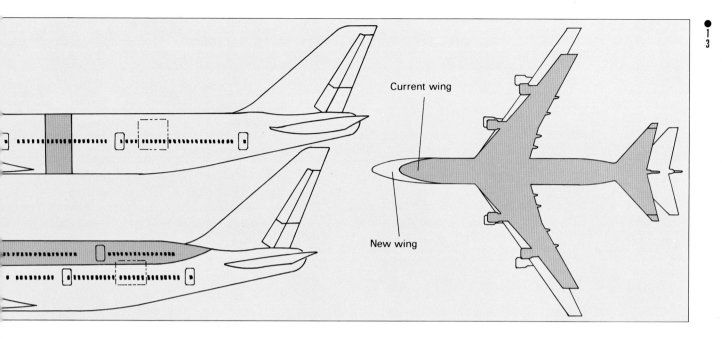

Current wing

New wing

noteworthy. There is also a specially converted airframe which transports a Space Shuttle on its fuselage.

The extended upper-deck 747-300 is presently considered to be the mainstream of 747 production, but how much further will the design evolve?

The 747 started off with maximum take-off weight of 710 000 lb (322 000 kg), and this has now been increased by 17 per cent to 833 000 lb (377 850 kg). A heavier airframe than this is already technologically difficult unless new, larger wings can be offered. Boeing has been studying the possibility of replacing the present 195 ft (59.44 m) span wing by a new wing with a span of 240–260 ft (73–79 m). This wing also would have reduced sweepback and greater aspect ratio. With such new wings, incorporating aerodynamic improvements, the fuselage could be further enlarged while retaining present performance. The 747 of the future is thus expected to achieve a 19-29 per cent fuel reduction per passenger compared with the -300 series, and a 45-55 per cent fuel saving compared with the -100 series.

Several proposals are under review for enlarging the fuselage. One stretches the present fuselage at two points, increasing passenger capacity to 550–650. Another method is extension of the upper deck through to the tail, giving a two-storeyed construction. If the present width of the upper deck is maintained, in six-abreast seat configuration, a total of 600–750 seats is possible. If the upper deck is widened to match that of the 767, total seating capacity increases to 700–800, with two aisles and seven seats across the width.

Only a rise in passenger traffic can justify the enormous investment needed for such a development. At the earliest such enlargement would take place in the late 1980s. It might come as late as 1990. However, there are no other plans for a new generation of giant passenger aircraft superior to the 747. The 747 may well keep growing and the 21st century will surely see these new 747s still in active use.

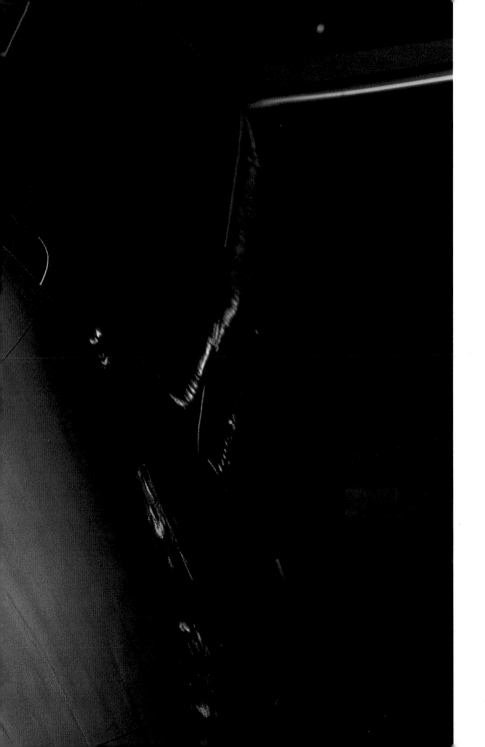

A challenge to greatness

The sheer size of the Boeing 747 is impressive. It has an overall length of 231 ft 4 in (70.51 m) and a wing span of 195 ft 8 in (59.64 m). The height to the top of the fin is 63 ft 5 in (19.33 m), almost as high as a five-storey building.

Its weight varies slightly, depending on series and type. The 747-200B has an operating empty weight of 367 000–377 000 lb and a maximum take-off weight of 833 000 lb (377 850 kg).

This gigantic structure cruises fast, at a top speed of about 490 kt (910 km/h) a cruising altitude of 35 000 ft (10 700 m). The cruise distance exceeds 5500 nm (10 200 km) with a full load of passengers and cargo, and 7000 nm (12 950 km) can be covered with a reduced load.

De Havilland's Comet I, the world's first production jet-engined passenger aircraft, made its debut in 1949, some 20 years before the 747 was launched. The Comet I cruised at 425 kt (785 km/h), for a distance of 1500 nm (2800 km), carrying 36-44 passengers.

Boeing, famed as the producer of great bombers such as the B-47 and B-52, turned out its range of jet airliners; the four-engined 707, three-engined 727, and the twin-engined 737, thereby gaining a great deal of experience in this field. The 747 stands as the climax of its technological achievement.

The 747 is a heavyweight giant from every angle. With the exception of the cockpit section, which is kept slender to ensure good visibility for the pilots, the fuselage is so swollen that the upper deck alone has a cabin space as large as that of smaller passenger aeroplanes. The windshield wipers work similarly to those of an automobile and the square visible on the upper cockpit wall is an emergency exit for the crew.

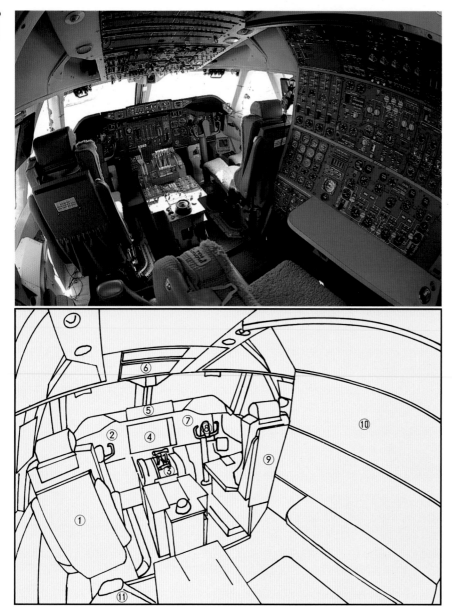

Cockpit

Compared with the overall size of the Boeing 747, its cockpit is very small. To facilitate better co-ordination between the crew, the seats are kept close together. Between the side-windows and the pilots' seats there is space to allow the pilot a clear view to the side and rear. The cockpit is situated above the main passenger deck, so that the same fuselage can be used for cargo transport, containers being loaded into the nose.

First generation long-range jet aircraft, such as the Boeing 707 and the Douglas DC-8, are manned by a crew of four. The Boeing 747 requires only two pilots and one flight engineer, as the navigation equipment makes a navigator unnecessary.

The Boeing Company was the first to apply the Inertial Navigation System (INS) to commercial transport aircraft. The INS enables aircraft to make long-range overwater flights without any assistance from outside the aircraft and without the skills of a navigator. In addition to INS, Boeing have introduced other advanced technologies, such as the improved autothrottle and Performance Management System (PMS).

The cockpit arrangement is for a crew of three: (1) captain's seat, (2) captain's main instrument panel, (3) throttles, (4) centre instrument panel, (5) auto-pilot mode selector panel, (6) overhead panel, (7) first officer's instrument panel, (8) control yoke, (9) first officer's seat (10) flight engineer's panel, (11) flight engineer's seat.

(Right) Cockpit positions for the captain (left) and first officer (right)

There is little new on the 747 instrument panel. It resembles that found on most jet airliners.

In front of the two pilot's seats are an identical set of instruments: the ADI (attitude direction indicator) and HSI (horizontal situation indicator) are in the centre, with the air speed indicator and radio direction indicator to the left, and the radar altimeter, ordinary altimeter, vertical speed indicator and clock to the right.

The central panel is mounted with instruments related to the engines, master warning displays, etc.

One new item in the 747 cockpit is a keyboard on each side of the central control stand. This is the INS (inertial navigation system), used for the input of flight data and for control. If the aircraft's latitude and longitude are fed in before take-off, the system calculates the speed and distance travelled on the basis of acceleration, automatically displays the track, and feeds such data to the autopilot and ADI, which guides the aeroplane to its destination.

In long-range airliners the cockpit crew used to comprise two pilots, a flight engineer and a navigator. With automated flight a reality, the 747 needs a crew of only three, disposing of the navigator.

(Left) Four main instruments in front of the pilot's seat; (right, above) the ADI, which shows the position of the aircraft and displays the signals for maintaining course; (right, below) the HSI, which indicates direction, deviation from the selected route, distance to the destination, etc; (left, above) the air speed indicator, which gives speed in knots – the Mach number is also shown; (left, below) the radio direction indicator.

(Above right) Engine instruments in the central panel are usually of the dial type, but some 747s use instruments which read vertically.

(Above, far right) The flight engineer's seat, surrounded by numerous instruments and switches.

(Right) The throttle levers are positioned between the pilots' seats. Pushing them forward increases power.

(Far right) The control column.

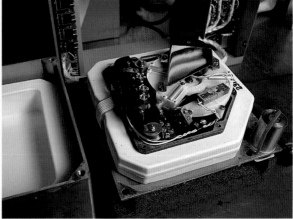

Gigantic airframe

The Boeing 747 has a wide fuselage, 225 ft 2 in (68.63 m) long and 21 ft 3.5 in (6.49 m) in outside diameter. In post-war civil aviation, the popular Douglas DC-4 and DC-7 piston-engined airliners had a fuselage width of 8 ft 1 in (2.46 m). Although this dimension remained unchanged, the DC series fuselage was gradually lengthened from the DC-4's 93 ft 5 in (28.47 m) to the final DC-7's 112 ft 7 in (34.32 m).

Stretching a fuselage had its limitations. To give even greater passenger capacity it was necessary to make the fuselage wider. Boeing's first jet airliner, the 707, had a fuselage width of 12 ft 4 in (3.76 m). Boeing then made the bold move of increasing fuselage width to 21 ft 3.5 in (6.49 m) in the 747, and in so doing popularized the term 'wide-bodied'.

The cost of a 747 is commensurate with its great size. At the time Boeing went in search of orders, in 1966, a 747-100 cost about US$18.5 million, double the price of a DC-8-61, then the world's largest passenger aeroplane. The newer model 747-300, which boasts a higher capacity than the earlier versions, is now priced at something like US$80 million.

Facing page
(Above left) The control panel for the performance management system (PMS), now standard equipment on modern passenger aircraft, automatically controls the course of flight, altitude, engine thrust, etc, by interfacing the autopilot and navigation systems with a computer. The 747 was not equipped with a PMS initially, but as it was instrumental in saving fuel, more 747s are now so equipped.

(Above centre) Control and display panel for INS.

(Above right) The gyro, the heart of INS.

(Right) Radar, the eyes of the aircraft.

(Below left) The flight data recorder, which stores all details of a flight, is used to analyse the causes of an accident.

(Below right) The voice recorder records all conversations in the cockpit. Both recorders are built to withstand the impact of a crash, fire, and water pressure.

This page
A 747SP used by Iraqi Air.

Spacious cabin

To many travellers an aeroplane is just a means of moving from one place to another. However, comfort on long journeys is of vital importance. The design staff in charge of interior work suffered certain constraints with the 707 and DC-8 due to the restricted cabin width of 11 ft 6 in (3.5 m). This allowed only a single central aisle dividing the seat rows.

The 747 cabin, with a fuselage width of 20 ft 1.5 in (6.13 m) at its widest point allows two aisles to divide the seats, dramatically changing the cabin's appearance. Two aisles had to be provided for in the wide-bodied 747 an aisle is required for every three seats under air safety regulations. Passenger traffic and serviceability also necessitated twin aisles and with lateral aisles across the fuselage at several points, greater freedom of passenger movement has been achieved.

The high 8 ft 4 in (2.54 m) ceiling, neatly finished with covered stowage, also enhances overhead clearance and gives the cabin an air of spaciousness.

Facing page
In the spacious two-aisle cabin of the 747, seat configuration varies with leg space and seat width.

(Top left) First class
(Top right) Business class
(Below) Economy class

This page
(Top left) An entrance door has a height of 6 ft 4 in (1.93 m) and a width of 3 ft 6 in (0.94 m), dimensions larger than those of ordinary aircraft.

(Top right) The emergency oxygen system is contained in the covered cabinet overhead. When the cabin is despressurised during flight oxygen masks drop automatically, ready for use.

(Below left) Galleys are fitted according to airlines' specific requirements. A typical international flight configuration has three locations in the cabin and one on the upper deck, though this arrangement differs from company to company.

(Below right) There is no standard number of lavatories on board. Aircraft on long-range routes usually have an average of 13, while short-range 747SRs may have fewer, between 9 and 11.

Fuselage structure

A fuselage under construction resembles the inside of a whale. Circular frames are placed 20 in (0.51 m) apart and are linked by stringers, set longitudinally at 8 to 10 in (0.2 to 0.25 m) intervals. Circular cross-sections are used, the better to withstand the stresses of cabin pressurisation.

The fuselage of the Boeing 747 is not completely circular. The frames for the top part of the fuselage are semicircular. However, the lower part, which is deeper, makes the fuselage 255.5 in (6.49 m) wide and 267.5 in (6.79 m) deep. Outer panels, ranging in size from 8 × 22 ft (6.71 m) to 30 × 20 ft (6.1 m), are welded to the frames. The panels have a minimum thickness of 0.062 in (1.6 mm).

For passenger-carrying 747s, the main deck is used as the passenger cabin and the lower deck serves as a cargo hold owing to the shape of the lower part of the fuselage. The floor for the main deck is 2 ft 7 in (0.79 m) below the top half of the fuselage. This makes the vertical height of the main deck greater than the depth of the lower deck, increasing the width and height of the passenger cabin. The cabins of new wide-bodied aircraft, such as the DC-10 and L-1011 have less space because their fuselages are completely circular. Although there is wiring and piping in the ceiling of the main cabin, it appears uneconomical to have so much unused space, but this is unavoidable for all wide-bodied transports that require maximum width in the passenger cabin. Any increase to the width of the present 747 fuselage would result in even more unused space, for the ceiling would be proportionally higher.

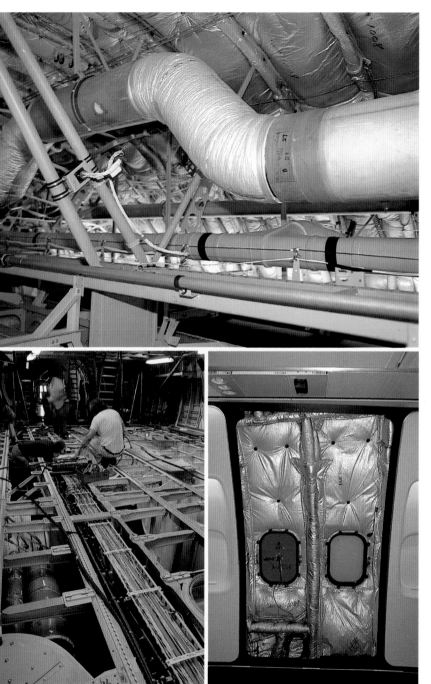

Facing page
(Top) Inside a 747 fuselage under construction.
Stringers are linked to frames. Two rows of
windows, for upper and main decks, can be seen.

(Bottom) Foundation structure is fabricated for
the cargo hold, one of the strongest parts of the
747. The hold can take 30 LD3 containers.

This page
(Top) Cabin air is fed along these pipes from the
engines, after temperature and pressure have
been lowered. The pressure in the cabin is
equivalent to 7000 ft (2130 m) altitude.

(Bottom left) Various pipes and wiring run under
the floor of the main deck. The deck structure is
covered with a honeycomb made of aluminium,
with titanium in areas under heavy load.

(Bottom right) Soundproof and heat resistant
insulation is installed under the skin. Fire
resistant panels are fixed to finish the cabin
interior.

Wings

The wing is one of the most important elements in determining the performance characteristics of an aeroplane. In the case of the 747, the main data are as follows: span 195 ft 8 in (59.64 m), area 5500 ft² (511.5 m²); sweepback angle at quarter chord 37.5 degrees; aspect ratio 6.96; taper ratio 0.356; wing thickness ratios, inboard 13.44 per cent, midspan 7.8 per cent, and outboard 8 per cent; dihedral angle 7 degrees; incidence 2 degrees.

These figures, which may not be extraordinary for a long-range passenger aircraft, are nevertheless significant from the design point of view. They affect the airfoil, the high-lift gear, the engine arrangements and the construction.

Wing area is a good example. Although the 747's maximum take-off weight is double that of the 707, its wing area is no more than 183 per cent of the 707's. In

other words wing loading, which means weight per square foot of wing area, has increased. In a giant aeroplane such as the 747, if wing loading is kept the same as that of a small machine, it follows that the structural weight increases, thereby decreasing the payload relative to the size of the airframe. A solution to this problem lies in increased wing loading. In the case of the 747 this is achieved by means of powerful high-lift gear, which enables the 747 to take off and land in the same runway length as that required by a 707.

It is the work of the wings that keeps an aircraft airborne. For landing, flaps are lowered to increase the lift. Powerful triple-slotted trailing edge flaps greatly enhance lift-off at low speeds.

The 747's wings are of box beam construction, comprising front/rear spars and top/bottom wing panels, to which leading and trailing edges are fixed. Multiple ribs are provided at almost right angles to the spars, and several stringers run continuously from the wing roots to their tips. The wing interior is sealed for use as an integral fuel tank. Each wing is made separately and coupled to the wing centre section, which passes through the fuselage.

This method of construction is common in jet airliners but the structural components of the 747 are much larger, with the root chord of 54 ft 4 in (16.56 m) reducing to 13 ft 4 in (4.06 m) at the tip. The wing skinning is noteworthy. Since the Boeing 727, it has become standard practice in US passenger aircraft to have seamless sheets covering the entire span of a wing, from root to tip.

In the case of the 747, three plates are rivetted on the topside and five plates on the underside between the front and rear spars, but their root-to-tip stretch along the wing is continuous and seamless, some plates being as long as 105 ft (32 m).

Wing panels vary in thickness, being about 0.35 in (9 mm) on the upper side and about 0.43 in (11 mm) on the underside, tapering down towards the wing tip to a thickness of about 0.08 in (2 mm).

Milling these huge plates and forming them to intricate curved shapes requires elaborate tooling incorporating the latest technology. Aircraft built in Europe and the USSR are heavier and more complicated to inspect and maintain because their plates are jointed, although the Airbus A300 relies on the same method of wing construction as the 747.

(Upper right) Stringers are rivetted on to the wing panels using a computer-operated machine tool.

(Upper far right) The undercarriage support beams are made of titanium to withstand the massive loading.

(Right) Assembly of the huge wing.

(Far right) The wing is about 7 ft (2.13 m) thick at the root and about 1 ft (0.3 m) thick at the tip. The slanting section receives the pylon from which an engine will be hung.

(Left) The process of mounting the wing.

High-lift gear

An important feature of super-sized aircraft such as the 747 is the powerful high-lift devices.

Boeing had previously developed a new type of triple-slotted trailing edge flap to enhance the take-off and landing performance of the 727. This resulted in smaller wings of reduced weight and drag. The 747's trailing edge flaps are also triple-slotted, the flaps being pushed out to the rear and 40 degrees downward.

In the 727 the leading edges are provided with slats to guide the air over the wing's upper surfaces, Kruger flaps being used only at the root. The 747 uses variable camber flaps which are pushed out from the wing's underside like Kruger flaps but also function as slats because of their aerodynamically efficient shape. There is a total of 13 leading edge flaps on each wing of the 747, three of which, placed inboard, are Kruger flaps.

The 747's flight controls are conventional. Lateral control is effected by the use of low-speed ailerons, operable only when the flaps are down, and high-speed ailerons located midway between the inboard and outboard trailing edge flaps, together with spoilers.

Control in pitch is through an elevator, and directional control is by rudder. All controls are operated hydraulically.

The incidence of the tailplane is adjustable through $(+)1° \sim -12°$ in order to trim the aircraft during flight.

(Far right) The wings during landing. Trailing edge flaps are brought fully down, with the spoilers up. Each wing has six spoilers, five of which, located outboard, are used together with ailerons for lateral control.

(Right, top and centre) Triple-slotted trailing edge flaps boost lift at take-off and landing.

(Right, bottom) Kruger flaps inboard of the wing leading edges.

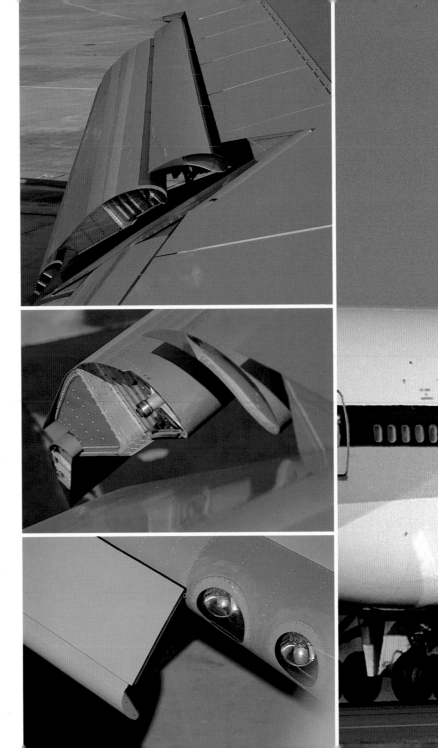

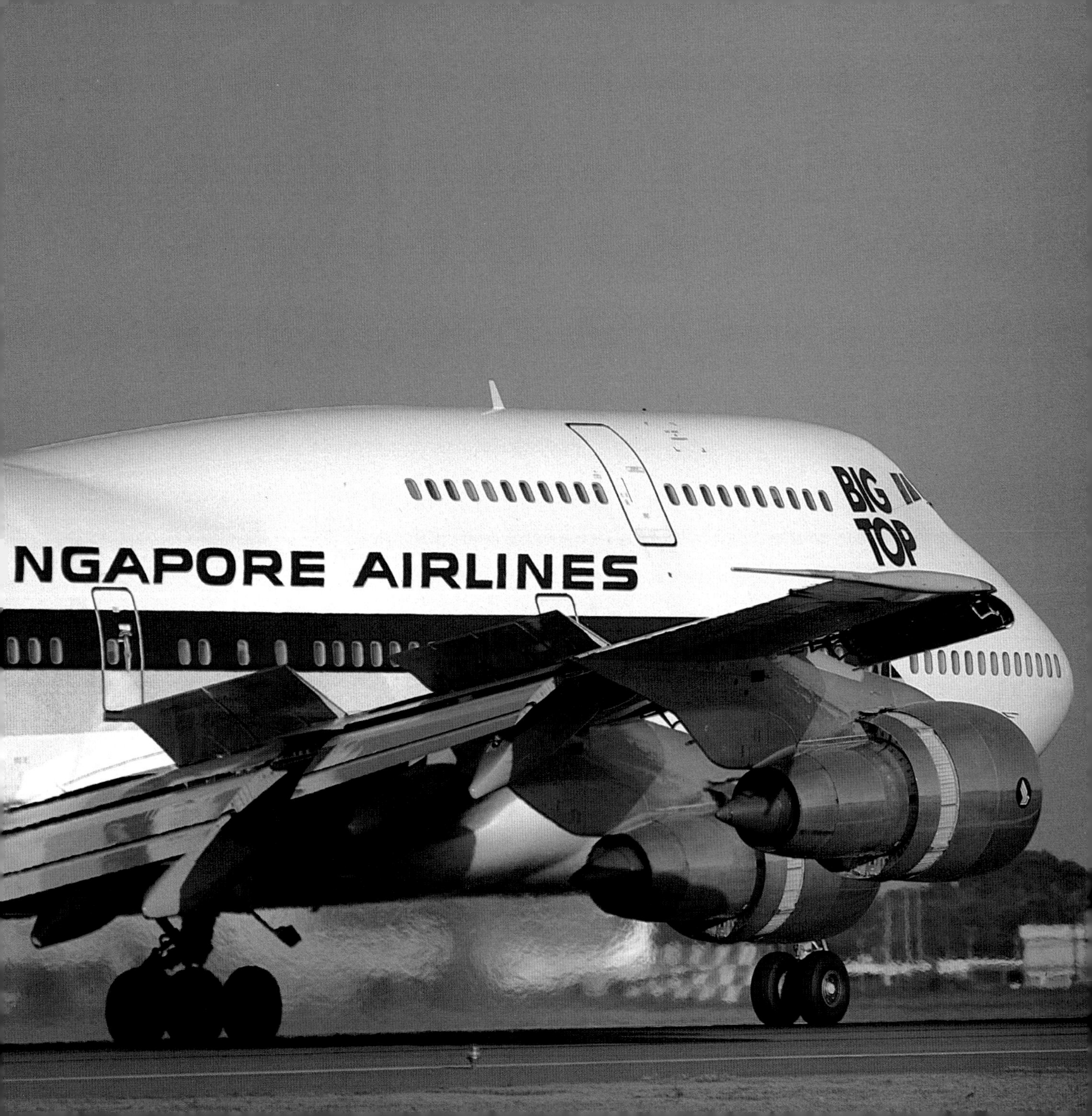
NGAPORE AIRLINES
BIG
TOP

Power plant

At present, three types of turbofan engine are fitted to the 747: Pratt and Whitney's JT9D, General Electric's CF6, and the Rolls-Royce RB.211. Initially the JT9D was the standard engine but Boeing responded to some airlines' desire to have the 747 powered by the CF6, used on the DC-10, and the RB.211, used on the L-1011.

These engines are all revolutionary power plants, with 200 per cent higher thrust, 20-25 per cent more efficient specific fuel consumption and far lower noise than those of the preceding generation. Widebodies such as the 747 could be conceived only because these new power plants were available.

Each of the engines originally had a thrust of about 45 000 lb (200 kN), which has now been increased to the order of 55 000 lb (245 kN). Fuel consumption has also been constantly improved, enhancing the 747's performance and economy.

The earlier variants had a fuel consumption of 0.35 lb/lb/hr (0.159 kg/kg/hr) at maximum take-off thrust (0.35 lb [0.159 kg] fuel consumed for 1 lb [1 kg] of thrust every hour, that is, 7 tons per hour for a thrust of 20 tons). Fuel consumption at the cruise, when about 20 per cent of the thrust is required, is 0.62 to 0.65 lb/lb/hr (0.28 to 0.295 kg/kg/hr).

More recent variants are recording a fuel consumption of 0.6 lb/lb/hr (0.272 kg/kg/hr) or lower – a remarkable achievement, considering that the figure for the JT3D on the 707 or DC-8 was around 0.74 (0.336).

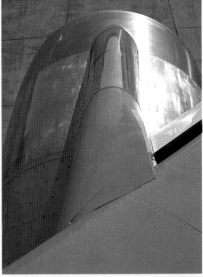

(Left) Pratt & Whitney's JT9D, one of the three types of turbofan engines used on the 747.

(Top) Engines are attached to the wings by means of pylons.

(Above) The large diameter of the fan contrasts with the jet exhausts, seen in the centre.

The three types of engine used on the 747 are large and generate high thrust. For instance, the JT9D-7R4D, a newer model of the JT9D series, is 132.7 in (3.37 m) long, 96.9 in (2.46 m) in diameter and weighs 8885 lb (4030 kg). Compared with the JT3D-7A used on the 707 and DC-8, which is 136.6 in (3.47 m) long, 53 in (1.35 m) in diameter and weighs 4340 lb (1970 kg), the JT9D-7R4D has a greater diameter for about the same length, and weighs twice as much. Its thrust is 54 750 lb (243 kN), nearly 2.9 times the JT3D-7A's 19 000 lb (84 kN).

Large fan diameter is a feature also shared by the CF6 and RB.211, even the smaller RB.211 having a diameter of 85.5 in (2.17 m). A larger fan is used to improve the bypass ratio over that of previous turbofan engines.

Turbofan engines were introduced in the early 1960s, their bypass ratio at that time being 0.6–1.5:1. They eventually replaced turbojet engines as main power plants for passenger aircraft. In the TF39 adopted for the US Air Force giant C-5 transport aircraft, a bypass ratio of 8:1 was achieved. This was followed by the development of three engines of great

bypass ratio and thrust for use on civil aircraft.

The bypass ratios of the JT9D, CF6, and RB.211 are 4.3–6:1, much lower than the TF39's 8:1. However, these ratios are still remarkable.

It is not only the improved bypass ratios that distinguish these superb engines. Thanks to the use of the latest technology, the compression ratio of air charged into the combustion chamber has been improved from the 17–20 of the previous engines to 25–30.

(Left) The fan of a CF6.

(Above) The high-pressure compressor of CF6 has 16 stages, in front of which there are six stages of stator vanes.

(Right) CF6 turbine blades.

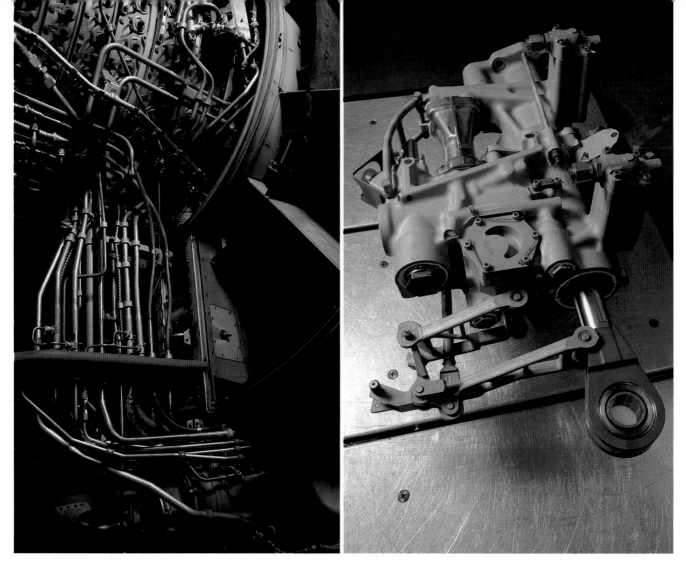

APU and hydraulic systems

When the aircraft is on the ground and the engines are not running, power for the various on-board controls and systems is supplied by an auxiliary power unit (APU) installed in the tail cone. This also functions as an auxiliary power source if an engine fails during flight.

All control surfaces except the leading edge flaps and landing gear are hydraulically operated. There are four independent hydraulic systems, and critical sections have double or triple oil lines.

Each engine is the power source for one hydraulic system, being linked to an engine-driven hydraulic pump and a high-pressure air-driven pump. In addition, two of the systems are also provided with an electrically-driven pump.

The 747's hydraulic backup systems are totally independent, so that failure of one system does not affect the flight controls. The control system will continue to operate even with two lines failing.

Electricity for cabin illumination, galleys, and so forth, and for the control

of systems is provided by the four 60 kVA generators, one to each engine. In addition two 60 kVA generators (or one of greater capacity on later models) are linked to the APU.

To pressurise and air-condition the cabins, high-pressure air is extracted from the compressor section of the engine. On the ground, the APU provides air-conditioning.

Hot air from the engines is also used to drive the leading edge flaps and to provide for the anti-icing of the main wings and the engine air intake sections.

Facing page
(Left) Each engine is fitted with a power generator and an hydraulic pump.

(Right) An hydraulic rudder actuator is employed for steering, which is too heavy to be manually operated.

This page
(Left) The APU fitted in the tail assembly supplies electricity and compressed air on the ground.

(Right) The APU is a gas turbine with an output of 1100 hp (820 kW).

Landing gear

As airframes grow, the landing gear presents a difficult design problem. It must sustain the weight, provide sufficient shock absorption, and spread the aircraft's load.

The 747 undercarriage comprises a twin-wheeled nose gear, a pair of four-wheeled main gear bogies at the roots of the main wings, and another pair on the underside of the fuselage. The 16 wheels of the main gear help to distribute the load. The bogies located on the fuselage underside are positioned to the rear of the wings, so that when the nose is lifted at take-off or landing they take the greater load. When the aircraft tilts, the bogies on either side are obviously subjected to a greater load.

The 747 has a shock absorbing system linking these two pairs of the main gear. This automatically compensates for the imbalance of load by means of oleo-pneumatic shock absorbers.

On ordinary passenger aircraft the ground steering system is connected to the nose gear only, but in the case of the 747 the fuselage side bogies are designed to turn in concert with the nose gear.

All wheels except the nose gear units are fitted with anti-skid disc brakes and the tyres are tubeless. All tyres are identical to facilitate interchangeability.

(Left) The 12.5-ton main landing gear consists of four steel legs to take the weight of a 747 at touch-down.

(Above) Double-wheeled nose is much lighter- weighing 1.4 tons.

Components

Not all 747 components are made by Boeing. In fact, a substantial portion is subcontracted. For instance, the fuselage is built by Northrop, the empennage by Vought, and the tailplane ailerons by Fairchild. About 70 per cent of the weight and 50 per cent of the work is contributed by about 1500 subcontractors, including secondary suppliers, some whom are overseas.

At Everett, the wings and the nose section are manufactured and assembled with all outside components to produce a complete aircraft.

In 1970, monthly 747 production reached seven, later falling to one aircraft per month. Demand picked up in 1978, and from mid-1979 to 1980 the former peak production of seven units per month was resumed. Since then the worldwide recession has reduced orders,

and in 1983 the production rate was down to 1.5 per month. However, there was no likelihood that production would be discontinued in the forseeable future.

Boeing's Everett plant was specially erected for 747 production. It is the world's largest factory, having a floor area of 3.5 million ft² (325 500 m²), and stands almost ten storeys high.

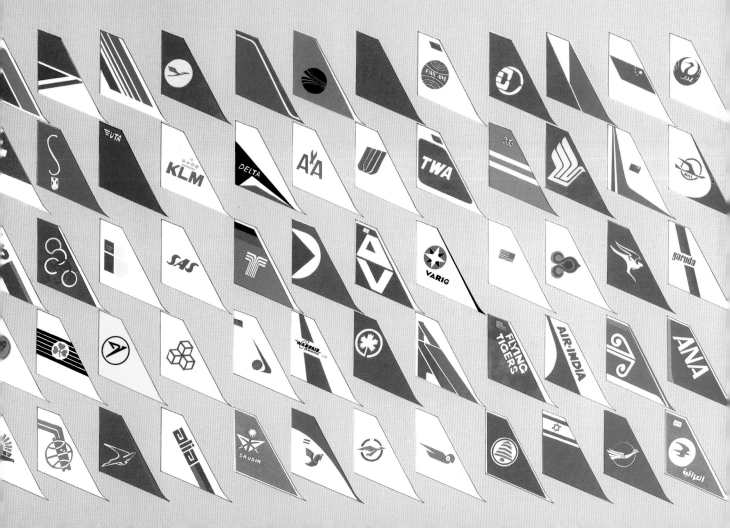

Asia and Oceania

Japan Air Lines

In the period following the Second World War Japan was prohibited from all aeronautical activities. Not until 1951 was Japan Air Lines approved as the first post-war Japanese airline. Initially it was operated by Northwest Airlines, and served only domestic routes, but in October 1952 it became self-contained, with its own aircraft. By this time the Japanese Government had decided to nominate and assist only one company to fly international routes. By 1953 Japan Air Lines had been reorganized, with 50 per cent of its capital (subsequently reducing to 44.3 per cent) coming from the national treasury.

While serving trunk routes in the domestic network, Japan's flag carrier also started expanding globally with the opening of the Tokyo-San Francisco service in February 1954. Its impressive growth is illustrated by the rise of JAL among the International Air Transport Association (IATA) members from eleventh position in 1965 to second position in 1982.

In addition to its domestic network, JAL's routes have been extended to cover Asia, Oceania, the Middle East, Europe and North and South America. In fact Africa is the only continent currently outside JAL's orbit.

JAL placed its first 747 order in June 1966, and commenced its trans-Pacific services in July 1970. It is the world's largest operator of 747s, having 41 in its own fleet, two on loan to Japan Asia Airways, four on order and more to be added in the future.

In fact, Africa is the only continent currently outside JAL's orbit.

JAL placed its first 747 order in June 1966, and commenced its trans-Pacific services in July 1970. It is the world's largest operator user of 747s, having 41 in its own fleet, two on loan to Japan Asia Airways, four on order and more to be added in the future.

In September 1983 JAL's active fleet consisted of 41 Boeing 747s, 20 DC-10s, 17 DC-8-61/62s and two Boeing 727s. The latest model ordered is the 747-300 with the extended upper deck, making a total of five variants, with the 747-100, -200B, SR, and F in service with the airline.

Of particular interest is 747SR, the short-range variant which had a seating capacity of 460 when first put into operation in 1973. Seating was subsequently increased to 498, and, in some cases, further expanded to 550 from 1980, making it the world's highest-capacity airliner.

Also, two of JAL's 747-200Bs have an extra tank to increase fuel capacity from 158.8 to 164.1 tons, thereby enabling non-stop direct flights between Tokyo and New York.

(Right) A JAL 747F with its nose raised to take on cargo.

Japan Asia Airways

In 1974 Japan Air Lines' decision to fly to the Chinese mainland was opposed by Taiwan, and this led to the discontinuation of the Japan-Taiwan service. Following negotiations, an agreement was reached for re-opening the Taiwan route, and to eliminate all political implications Japan Asia Airways was created in 1975 as a wholly-owned subsidiary of Japan Air Lines.

At the outset JAA served the Tokyo-Taipei route only, but then added other services from Osaka and Okinawa. It now also flies to Hong Kong and Manila.

The airline owns three DC-8-61s in addition to two 747s on lease from JAL.

All Nippon Airways

ANA was born in 1957 by the merger of Japan Helicopter and Airplane Transport and Far Eastern Airlines, both of whom had operated domestic services since 1952. ANA subsequently absorbed Fujita Airlines in 1963 and Nakanihon Air Services in 1965, and it acquired the regular service of Nagasaki Airlines in 1967.

ANA made great strides in line with Japan's economic growth. The change to jets was initiated by Boeing's 727-100, which entered service in 1964. It then introduced the smaller 737 for local service, at the same time replacing the 727-100 with the longer-fuselaged 727-200. To cope with an ever-increasing demand, ANA then added 21 L-1011s and 15 747SRs.

The number of passengers carried by ANA exceeds that of JAL, having totalled some 200 million in 1981. The airline boasts the widest coverage within Japan. In 1971 ANA also began short-range international charter flights extending to Hong Kong, Manila, Singapore, Beijing, and Shanghai.

Korean Air Lines

Korean Air Lines was established as a national carrier in 1962 by the re-organisation of Korean National Airlines and reverted to private status in 1969.

The airline was among the first in Asia to introduce 747s, following JAL and India Air. It now has a fleet of ten 747-200Bs, four 747-200Fs and two SPs. It

(Top) KAL 747-200B

(Above left) KAL 747-200F bearing the insignia 'Korean Air Cargo'.

(Above right) CAAC 747SP.

also owns DC-10s and A300s, covering three of the four widebodied types.

CAAC (Civil Aviation Administration of China)

Formed in 1949, CAAC undertakes not only air transport but agricultural aviation, aerial survey, resources exploration, and all civil aviation activities.

For some years CAAC used Soviet aircraft, together with British Viscounts and Tridents. After the re-establishment

of ties with the USA, CAAC started using Boeing 707s. It now uses three 747SPs for long-distance transport, and has placed a further order for two SPs and one -200B.

CAAC operates various overseas routes in Asia, Africa, Europe, and North America, as well as the domestic network.

China Airlines

This Taiwanese airline goes back to 1959, when it was engaged in charter flights and cargo transport. In 1962 it began scheduled services on Taiwan's domestic routes.

Taiwan also has another airline, Civil Air Transport, which originally took charge of international routes, operating with US capital. In 1966 China Airlines

went into international service, changing roles with Civil Air Transport, which in 1968 came to specialise in charter flights as Taiwan's domestic airline.

China Airlines' adoption of jet aircraft began with Boeing 727s for the Southeast Asian route. These were followed by Boeing 707s to open the American service. Its equipment now includes one 747-100, three 747-200s and two SPs.

Philippine Airlines

Established in 1941, PAL resumed operations in 1946 following their suspension during the Second World War.

In 1947 it became the first Southeast Asian airline to fly to London, but in 1954 PAL reduced its external services to concentrate on the domestic network. In 1962 it ventured once again into international services.

McDonnell Douglas DC-8s and then DC-10s were adopted for the international routes, followed by 747 and A300. PA has four 747-200Bs.

Although PA was a private company at its inception, the Philippine Government came to own 54 per cent of the shares and nationalised the airline in 1977, with 99.7 per cent control.

Malaysian Airline System

Originally formed as Malayan Airways under British rule in 1947, the airline was renamed Malaysian Airways in 1963, when Malaysia became a new nation with the amalgamation of Malaya, Singapore, Sabah and Sarawak. With the independence of Singapore in 1965, it was reorganised as Malaysia-Singapore Airlines. In 1972 Malaysia set up a national company under the title Malaysian Airline System.

In addition to its domestic network and routes in Southeast Asia, MAS flies to Australia, the Middle East and Europe. It has two 747-200Bs.

Singapore Airlines

A nationally owned company born out of the separation of Malaysia and Singapore in 1975, SIA took over a major portion of the international network of Malaysia-Singapore Airlines, with regular services covering Asia, Europe and North America, and operating on a larger scale than MAS.

Apart from 16 747-200Bs, SIA ordered eight -300s with the extended upper deck, and these entered service in 1983.

Pakistan International Airlines

Formed in 1951, PIA commenced operation in 1954 and took over Orient Airways, which had been active before separation from India, to become the present company. Its widespread international network is flown by two 747-200Bs and two -200 Combis.

Cathay Pacific Airways

This Hong Kong-based airline enjoys wide coverage of Asia and Oceania, and operates services to London via the Middle East. Its equipment has included DC-4s, DC-6s, Electras, and Convair 880s. Boeing 707s and L-1011 TriStars were the main equipment, and then 747s were added. Cathay now has seven 747-200Bs and one -200F cargo freighter.

Thai Airways International

Thai Airways international operation began in 1959 as a joint venture with SAS but the latter relinquished management participation in 1977 in favour of an advisory role. Thai Airways is now particularly active on the competitive trans-Pacific route.

Its fleet comprises DC-8s, DC-10s and A300s, plus six 747-200Bs.

Air India

Air India was born in 1946 as the successor to Tata Airlines, which had been active since 1932 and in 1953 was nationalised, leaving domestic services to Indian Airlines. Air India is devoted to international services and owns ten 747-200Bs.

Garuda Indonesian Airways

Founded in 1950 as a 50/50 joint-venture with KLM, Garuda came under full control of the Indonesian Government in 1954. In its fleet, which includes F-28s, DC-9s, DC-10s and A300s, are six 747-200Bs, extending its service beyond Asia and Oceania to Europe.

Qantas Airways

Dating back to 1920, this company was known as Qantas Empire Airways during 1934-1967. Qantas was the first airline to establish a round-the-world passenger route, in 1958. It has streamlined its fleet with 747s and owns 25 altogether, including SPs.

Air New Zealand

The predecessor of Air New Zealand, Tasman Empire Airways, began operation in 1940 between Australia and New Zealand. Originally owned jointly by New Zealand, Australian and UK interests, Air New Zealand became the national flag-carrier in 1961. In 1965 it went beyond Oceania with a service to the USA, and changed its name from TEA to Air New Zealand.

Air New Zealand now serves the entire Pacific basin including Japan, the United States and Australia and, since 1978, domestic routes acquired by the absorbtion of New Zealand National Airways.

On long-distance routes it uses DC-8s, Boeing 707s, and DC-10s. It is now replacing these with 747s, and owns five -200Bs.

North and South America

Pan American World Airways

Formed in 1927, this well-known United States carrier monopolised many international routes in pre-war days. Following its inauguration of South American services, it opened the Pacific service to Manila in 1935 and the transatlantic service to Europe in 1939.

Despite the loss of its monopolistic international position after the Second World War, when most overseas routes were opened to other airlines, Pan Am continued to stretch its network across the world. Pan Am was the very first airline to order the Boeing 707, paving the way for the jet age and ultimately giving Boeing the momentum for development of the 747. It was also Pan Am which inaugurated a direct New York-Tokyo service with 747SPs.

On international routes Pan Am is less powerful now that other airlines are competing, but domestically it has expanded further with the acquisition of National Airlines in 1980.

A prime user of the 747 it has a fleet of 44 of all variants, but has given up first place to JAL.

Northwest Airlines

In 1926 Northwest Airlines started
operations as a postal carrier, and began
passenger services in the following year.
By 1945 the company had grown to
operate the transcontinental route.

However, the real take-off had to wait
until the end of the Second World War,
when Northwest was granted permission
to operate the northern Pacific service

linking the Far East and Alaska. For
many years this route was held almost
exclusively by Northwest Airlines, to
such an extent that they rightly called
themselves Northwest-Orient Airlines.

Subsequently, Northwest Airlines
acquired the right to fly the trans-Pacific
route from the USA to Asian destinations
via Hawaii. It is currently ranked among
the top airlines, rivalling Pan Am and

JAL in the Pacific zone, and has also
expanded its network to include services
to Europe.

In the piston era Northwest Airlines
used DC-4s and DC-7s. With the advent
of jet airliners, DC-8s, and Boeing 707s
were adopted, to be succeeded by 747s
and DC-10s. The airline now has a total
of 29 747s, comprising -100s, -200Bs,
and -200Fs.

Trans World Airlines

The abbreviation for Trans World Airlines, TWA, originally stood for Transcontinental and Western Air, founded in
1929. The former TWA was an amalgamation of Western Air Express, organised
as a core company in 1926, with Transcontinental Air Transport and Pittsburgh
Aviation Industries. TWA grew to be
capable of developing its own specifi-
cations for aircraft, and these were
realised as the historic Douglas DC-1
and DC-2.

In 1939 Howard Hughes acquired
management control and the company
co-operated with Lockheed in the development of the Constellation four-
engined passenger aircraft.

The change of name to Trans World
Airlines in 1950 reflected the expansion
overseas which has made TWA one of
the world's largest airlines. TWA was
second only to Pan Am in ordering 747s,
and its fleet now comprises 15 -100s and
three SPs. The total number of 747s is
not considered large for the company's
size. This is because TWA, jointly with
Eastern Air Lines, has a commitment
with Lockheed for a large number of
L-1011s.

United Airlines

Discounting Aeroflot, UAL is the world's largest airline, its 300-aircraft fleet including 18 747-100s.

Its origins go back to 1931, when five companies, including Boeing Air Transport, Varney Air Lines, and National Air Transport, amalgamated under the present name. One of the 'big four' in the USA, UAL has grown shoulder-to-shoulder with American Airlines, Eastern Air Lines, and TWA.

While its competitors expanded overseas after the Second World War, UAL concentrated on reinforcing its domestic network. With the absorption of Capital Airlines in 1981 its scale of operation became comparable with those of its rivals.

UAL's domestic services link more than 100 cities. Until recently international routes were confined to Canada and Mexico, but in 1983 UAL opened a Pacific route to Japan.

The relatively small number of 747s held by UAL is explained by its lack of long-range services. UAL was the first to fly Boeing 767s, the newly-born successor to some one hundred 727s which it operates.

Continental Airlines

Continental served the local network in Midwest USA until 1957, when the Chicago-Los Angeles service began, using a DC-7B. It subsequently became a trunk route operator and now also flies to Micronesia and Japan. Four 747-100s were bought and commissioned into domestic service following purchases by TWA and American, although all were later sold and replaced by DC-10s.

Delta Air Lines

Delta Air Service was founded in 1925 as a pioneer aerial cropdusting company and began modest passenger transport operations in 1929. The airline took advantage of the removal of the monopolisation by Eastern Air Lines of the Miami and Chicago routes in 1945, and thereafter made rapid progress. In 1953, upon merger with Chicago and Southern Air Lines, its name was changed to Delta C+S Air Lines. It assumed its present name in 1956 and in 1972 absorbed Northeast Airlines.

Five 747s were purchased by Delta, but these were resold and its fleet now consists mainly of L-1011s.

Braniff Airways

Formed in 1928, Braniff's heyday occurred in the 1960s, when its aircraft were painted in rainbow colours to attract publicity and business. However, from the end of the 1970s its overstretched network and escalating fare competition led the company to bankruptcy in May 1982. It had one 747-100, one -200B and three SPs.

American Airlines

Formed in 1930 by the merger of Colonial, Universal, Southern, and several other airlines, American was initially named American Airways and changed to its present title in 1934.

Its international services are presently limited to destinations in Canada, Central America, and the Caribbean, and no flights across the Atlantic are offered.

Eight 747-100s and six -100Fs are owned.

NASA

Space Shuttles are launched in Florida, but they are built in California, where they usually land.

The problem of transporting these vehicles across the American continent has been overcome by the use of a converted 747, which carries a Space Shuttle on its back. In 1983 there was one 747 performing this role, but another was expected to be added.

Transamerica Airlines

This charter flight operator is a subsidiary of Transamerica, a conglomerate with controlling interests in finance, insurance, real estate, motion picture and car hire businesses. It was formed in 1948 as Los Angeles Air Service, renamed Trans International Airlines in 1960 and assumed its present title in 1979.

In 1976 it acquired leading charter flight company Saturn Airways to become the world's largest charter company. Transamerica Airlines ownes a fleet of some 40 aircraft, including three 747-200Cs.

Flying Tiger Line

Organised in 1925 as National Skyway Freight, the present name was adopted in 1947. In 1980 it absorbed Seaboard World Airlines and became one of the world's top cargo carriers. Three 747-100Fs and ten -200Fs are operated.

World Airways

A charter flight company formed in 1948, World Airways began operating domestic and international passenger services in 1979, mainly with DC-10s, although it also has two 747-200Cs.

US Air Force

The US Air Force has four 747s serving as airborne command post E-4s, with two more due to be added as a defensive measure against nuclear warfare. They carry various communications equipment and are equipped for in-flight refuelling.

CP Air

In 1968 Canadian Pacific Air Lines changed its name to CP Air. It was founded in 1942, when Canadian Pacific Railways took the lead in consolidating Canadian Airlines, established in 1926, and nine other small airlines serving local communities.

For a period after the Second World War CP Air continued to serve the local network only, but in 1949 it opened an international route to Australia via Hawaii and Fiji. This was followed in the same year by the commencement of a service to Tokyo and Hong Kong. Having become recognised as a leading international airline, CP Air then decided to relinquish its domestic services.

The airline has used 747s since 1973, and has four -200Bs in its fleet at present.

Air Canada

Formed as Trans-Canada Airlines in 1937, as a wholly-owned subsidiary of Canadian National Railways, Air Canada took its present form in 1965 and was denationalised in 1978. Apart from domestic networks, it also operates services to the USA, Central America, and Europe, using five 747-100s and two -200 Combis.

Wardair Canada

This international charter flight operator has four 747s, both -100 and -200B variants, as well as two DC-10s.

From a humble start as Polaris Charter in 1946, with one Fox Moth biplane, Wardair has made a remarkable progress. The company takes its name from its founder, Mr Ward.

Avianca

The national airline of Colombia boasts the longest history in the North and South Americas, having originated from SCADTA, founded in 1919. In addition to its domestic network, Avianca also operates services to North and South America and Europe. Five 747s are owned, comprising the -100, -100F and -200 variants.

Aerolineas Argentinas

Argentine's flag carrier was established by consolidating four airlines. It is now the second largest airline in South America behind the Brazilian operator Varig. Its international services cover North America, Europe and South Africa, using six 747-200s and one SP.

Varig

Viacao Aerea Rio-Grandense (Varig) was formed in 1927 and initially operated in southern Brazil only. It gradually expanded its services, merged with Aereo Geral in 1951 and introduced a direct service to New York in the same year.

A great expansion of Varig was prompted by the absorbtion of Real in 1961. This allowed Varig to take over various domestic routes, as well as international services extending to the USA, Mexico and Japan. Further expansion came in 1965, with the acquisition of Panair do Brazil and its European traffic rights.

Varig is now the largest operator in South America, with a wide coverage of the USA, Europe, Asia, and Africa. The first jet airliner adopted by Varig was the French Caravelle, later supplemented by the Boeing 707 and Convair 990. At present its fleet comprises Boeing 707s, 727s, 737s, Douglas DC-10s, and Airbus A300s, to which three Boeing 747-200 Combis have been added.

Swissair

Swissair was born in 1931 from the merger of Ad Astra Aero, formed in 1919 and Balair, formed in 1925. Its main equipment at that time was the Dutch-built Fokker-F.VII/3m.

In 1932 Swissair became the first European company to use an American aeroplane. This was the Lockheed Orion, a small four-seater which flew over 60 mph faster than the aircraft of the rival airlines.

After the Second World War its fleet comprised Douglas DC-4, DC-6, DC-7 and DC-8 airliners, together with Convair 240s, 990s, and Caravelles. The 747, which entered service with the airline in 1971, was the first Boeing aircraft to be adopted by Swissair. As DC-10s formed the mainstay of its fleet, the number of 747s was limited to two, but the airline turned to the -300 as soon as it became available and now has five.

Incidentally, Swissair was the first user of the DC-9-50 and -80, and was the first, with Lufthansa, to order the Airbus A310. The airline is 75 per cent privately-owned.

British Airways

Europe's largest airline was formed in September 1972 by the merger of British Overseas Airways Corporation (BOAC) and British European Airways (BEA), and commenced formal operation in April 1974 upon consolidation of the respective services.

BOAC had a history going back to 1919, the year in which several airlines started commercial transport and scheduled passenger services between London and Paris. Under the British Government's guidance, with a view to fostering a strong airline, four companies joined hands in 1924 to give birth to Imperial Airways. Subsidised by the Government, the company expanded its network across the British Empire, linking Australia, Hong Kong, and Capetown in South Africa. Most large passenger aircraft built in Great Britain before the last war were developed to meet Imperial Airways' requirements.

Meanwhile, several airlines were consolidated in 1935 and British Airways was created to compete with Imperial Airways on European services. The Government intervened, and further consolidation led to the formation of BOAC, a nationalised company, in November 1939. BOAC, which took an active part in military transport during the war, expanded its network worldwide.

BEA was formed in August 1946, as another national company, to consolidate the European services of BOAC with those of several smaller airlines. Although BEA was principally intended to serve Europe, it had actually extended its services to such cities as Moscow, Istanbul, and Tel Aviv by the time the merger of BOAC and BEA took place.

The growth of British Airways illustrates the history of British civil air transport, which took the lead in the commercial aviation in 1952 by commencing regular services with the Comet I, the world's first jet-engined passenger aeroplane, and in 1976 by operating, jointly with Air France, the world's first supersonic passenger service, using Concorde.

At present its fleet of 747s comprises 16 -100s and eight -200Bs, five examples joining the airline in 1970.

Air France

Civil aviation flourished all over Europe in 1919. In France many airlines were formed and grew through competition. Air France was born in 1933 by the amalgamation of five airlines, similar to the manner in which Britain's Imperial Airways was formed. A national company with a 25 per cent Government holding, it covered not only Europe but also the French colonies in Africa, the Far East and South America.

When France was under German occupation during the Second World War, the name Air France disappeared for a while, but was restored in January 1946. In September 1948 Government participation increased to 70 per cent (now 99 per cent), to make it fully nationalised. Since then, Air France has moved ahead to regain the important position in world civil aviation which it used to enjoy. Its strength is demonstrated by its quantity order to bring the A300 Airbus project to fruition.

Air France operates a fleet of some 100 aircraft, comprising the Boeing 727, 737, and 747, Concorde, and A300. Altogether 31 747s are owned, a mixture of -100s, -200s, and -200Fs.

UTA (Union de Transport Aériens)

While flag carrier Air France was re-organised after World War Two, several private airlines were also formed. Among them were TAI and UAT, which operated international services and merged in 1963 to become UTA. TAI was established in 1946, and mainly served the French colonies in Africa and Vietnam, opening a route to Los Angeles via New Zealand in 1960. UAT was founded in 1949 and operated African services.

UTA's current network primarily covers Africa, Asia, and the South Pacific, and in addition to scheduled services it also carries out chartered transport flights. Its aircraft include DC-8s, DC-10s, and 747s. The 747 family is made up of two -200 Combis, two -200Bs, and two -300s.

UTA Industries, a subsidiary of UTA, took out a license with Aero Spacelines of the USA to manufacture a super-sized freighter, Super Guppy, and produced it for Airbus Industrie. This aeroplane is operated by Aéromaritime, another UTA subsidiary.

KLM (Royal Dutch Airlines)

KLM is the only airline which has retained its original name since its foundation, in October 1919.

Its first service on the Amsterdam-London route began in May 1920 and many more European routes followed. In 1931 it flew to Batavia (now Jakarta) in Indonesia, and before the Second World War KLM carried more passengers than either Imperial Airways or Air France, mainly because it always kept its fleet up to date. KLM was the first airline in Europe to fly the Douglas DC-2 and DC-3.

Immediately after the war KLM took quick steps toward recovery by negotiating the lease of Douglas C-54s (the military version of the DC-4) from the US Government. Using this aircraft KLM reopened the Batavia route in November 1945.

One of the Europe's major airlines, KLM is now 74.9 per cent controlled by the Dutch Government.

The first of KLM's 747s was put into service in January 1971, and it has a fleet of 16.

Alitalia

Italy was no exception in consolidating airlines in prewar days. In 1934 a national company, Ala Littoria, was created to serve a wide network, eventually to be discontinued by the outbreak of war.

Italy was the first of the defeated axis powers to recommence air transport operations after the war. An Italian-British joint venture was formed in September 1946, with a 30 per cent BEA shareholding, to become Alitalia.

Domestic services commenced in May 1947 and were extended to European destinations. A South American route was opened in 1950.

In 1957 Alitalia absorbed Linee Aree Italiane, a similar joint-venture in which TWA had a 40 per cent holding, to become a 70 per cent Government-controlled flag carrier operating both domestic and international services.

Alitalia took itself into the jet age in 1960 by introducing the Caravelle and DC-8. In 1970 it commissioned a 747 into service, followed by DC-10s and A300s. Its 747 fleet comprises nine 747s: -200s, -200 Combis, and -200Fs.

Lufthansa German Airlines

Many German airlines which founded in 1919 were united on the Government's initiative in 1926 to become Lufthansa. The company served Europe, gradually extending to the Middle East and Far East, and adding an airmail service to South America. It held the position of top European airline until the outbreak of the Second World War.

After the war, when Germany was divided, Lufthansa was reborn in West Germany, commencing operations in 1955. Despite being ten years behind, it soon caught up with the other major carriers, becoming one of the top five Iata airlines by the mid-1960s.

Lufthansa was the first company in Europe to order the Boeing 727 and 737, and was second only to United States airlines in choosing the 747. Lufthansa flew its first 747 in April 1970. It now owns three -200s, ten -200 Combis and two -200Fs.

Condor Flugdienst

A Lufthansa subsidiary created in 1961 by the amalgamation of two charter service operators, Condor used to have one 747-200 in addition to its Boeing 727s and 707s. However this was transferred to Lufthansa and replaced by a DC-10.

SAS (Scandinavian Airlines System)

SAS was established in August 1946 by the airlines of Sweden, Denmark, and Norway, with the aim of operating joint international services. In 1950 it took over the domestic networks of the respective countries and became the representative airline of Scandinavia.

SAS became famous in 1954 when it introduced a route over the North Pole, linking Europe and the West Coast of the USA. In 1957 a new route connecting Europe and the Far East via Anchorage was pioneered. The airline operates to many parts of the world and has used four 747s since April 1971.

Sabena (Belgian World Airlines)

Formed in 1923 as a successor to SNETA, Sabena stretched its network after the war and became the first company in Europe to use the Boeing 707 on Atlantic services.

It began its first 747 operations at the end of 1970, and now has two -100s.

Cargolux Airlines International

Luxembourg established its airline in 1970. It is owned by a national company, Luxair, Icelandair and a Swedish Shipping company among others, and has one 747-200 and two -200Fs.

Iberia

Established in 1940, Iberia's services extend beyond the domestic network, to Europe, North and South America, the Middle East and Africa. It owns six -200Bs, which have been in service since late 1970.

Air Portugal (TAP)

Formed in 1944 as a division of the Civil Aviation Ministry, Air Portugal commenced operation in 1946. The Boeing 707 was introduced for long-range services in 1965. The 747 fleet, operated since 1972, consists of two -200s.

Aer Lingus

Formed in 1936, Aer Lingus started its Atlantic service in 1958 through sister company Aerlinte Eireann, using the name Aer Lingus for commercial reasons. It was later consolidated with Government capital. This small company operates two 747-100s.

Olympic Airways

In 1957 TAE (Greek National Airlines) was acquired by Aristotle Onassis, who renamed it Olympic Air. It subsequently became a national company in 1975. Two 747-200Bs are in its fleet.

Middle East and Africa

El Al Israel Airlines

In November 1948, soon after the foundation of Israel, El Al airline was formed, the majority of its funds coming from Government sources. Its services, which are primarily overseas flights, began with routes to London and Paris in 1949 using DC-4s. In 1950 El Al acquired Universal Airways of South Africa, together with its local network. In May 1951 a New York via London route was opened using the Constellation, making El Al the first non-European, non-American airline to fly across the Atlantic.

El Al continues to purchase new equipment in order to compete with the world's major airlines. It was only three days behind BOAC when the first long-range turbo-prop airliner, the Britannia, was put in service on the Atlantic route in December 1957. The 707 jetliner was first used in 1961, and it was the first Middle East airline to order 747s, which it put in operation in 1971. At present four -200s, two -200s, and one 200C are owned, along with Boeing 707s, 737s, and 767s.

Syrian Arab Airlines

Formed in December 1946, Syrian Airways depended, like many late-comers, on a leading airline (in this case, Pan Am) for technological advice and the loan of flight crews. It began operations in June 1947, using DC-3s, but suffered management problems and suspended activities the following year, when Pan Am withdrew.

Syrian Airways resumed operation in 1951 with Government support, but with no success in sight the Government ordered dissolution of the company. In 1954 a fresh start was made as a national company assuming the same name, which was eventually merged with Misrair of Egypt to form United Arab Airlines. It became independent again in September 1961, following Syria's sep-

aration from Egypt.

The company gradually expanded, and although quite a few aircraft were lost in the Middle East wars of 1967 and 1973, it kept up its network serving the Middle East, North Africa, Europe and Asia. Two 747 SPs are owned.

Iraqi Airways

Organised in December 1945 as a division of Iraqi National Railways, Iraqi Airways became an independent company in 1960. At present it has three 747-200Cs and one SP, in its fleet, which includes the 707, 727, 737 and the Russian Ilyushin Il-76 freighter.

Egyptair

This company originated as Misr Air-work, formed in 1932 and renamed Misrair in 1949. After Egypt and Syria formed the United Arab Republic the company merged with Syrian Arab Airlines in January 1961 to create United Arab Airlines. However, the United Arab Republic broke up in September of the same year and the new company split, the title United Arab Airlines being taken over by Egypt. The present name was adopted in 1971.

The current fleet consists mainly of Boeing 707s and Airbus A300s, but one secondhand 747-100 was acquired in 1983.

Saudia (Saudi Arabian Airlines)

This is the largest airline in the Middle East, having some 50 jet airliners including eight 747-100s, one -200F and two SPs. Other widebodies in the fleet are the L-1011 and A300.

Saudia was established by the Government at the end of 1946, with services confined for some time to the Middle East and North Africa. In 1967, operations to London heralded the start of international route extensions, later reaching Asia and the USA. The rapid growth of its fleet was especially remarkable after the oil crisis of 1973.

Middle East Airlines - Air Liban

This company's full name combines MEA and Air Liban, which were merged in 1965.

MEA was formed in 1945, and Pan Am took a 36 per cent shareholding in 1949. With support from BOAC, which became a proxy of Pan Am for a 49 per cent shareholding between 1955 and 1961, the airline grew to operate Comet 4Cs.

Air Liban was formed in 1945, with support from Air France, and started flying Caravelle jets over the international routes in the 1960s.

The merged company absorbed Lebanese International Airways in 1969. Its major shareholders are Intra Investment (62.5 per cent) and Air France (28.5 per cent). Unlike its Middle East competitors, governmental participation is included in its financial structure. It owns three 747-200 Combis.

Alia (The Royal Jordanian Airlines)

There were two airlines in Jordan, Arab Airways, formed in 1946, and Air Jordan, formed in 1950. In 1958 they were merged to become Air Jordan of Holyland. In 1960, with a partial Government holding, the airline was reorganised as Jordan Airways, which operated with only two Viscounts and one DC-3, yielding poor results.

Further Governmental support was given in 1963 to form the present company, operating on a limited scale. After complete nationalisation it grew to have about 20 jet transports, including one 747-200 and two -200 Combis.

Alia serves the Middle East and Western Europe, and also operates services to the USA and Southeast Asia.

Iran Air

Iran Air was organised as a flag carrier in 1962, by the amalgamation of Iranian Airways and Peruvian Air Service.

Formed in 1944, Iranian Airways initially operated domestic routes, but gradually expanded into its neighbouring countries and to Europe, without much success. Peruvian Air Service was formed in 1954 and specialised in freight and international passenger services, but suffered from financial difficulties. The Iranian Government therefore decided to reorganise them as a national company.

With support from Pan Am for fleet modernisation, it introduced the Boeing 727 in 1965. This was followed by the 707 in 1970, the 737 in 1971 and the 747SP in 1976. At present it owns one -100, five -200s and four SPs.

Iran Air's routes are concentrated in the Middle East and Europe, but it also operates regular services to Tokyo via Beijin. The 1978 revolution has brought a change in in-flight services. As with other Islamic nations, no alcohol is carried on board.

Iranian Air Force

The 747 was developed basically as a jetliner, but some have been converted for military uses, exemplified by the US Air Forces's E-4.

The Iranian Air Force's fleet of 12 747s comprises three special-purpose 747-100s with air refuelling capability, four -100s remodelled as freighters, and five -200F freighters.

The tanker models have a flying boom refuelling device similar to that adopted by the US Air Force. One of the largest tankers in the world, it is superior even to the KC-10 variant of the DC-10 or the Royal Air Force's L1011-500.

South African Airways

Africa's largest airline presently operates 16 747s: two -200 Combis, two -300s, and six SPs, in addition to Boeing 737s and Airbus A300s.

South African Airways has a history going back to 1929, when Union Airways was established by British investors. It was eventually purchased by the Government (before the independence of Republic of South Africa in 1961) and renamed SAA in 1934. The following year it absorbed Southwest African Airways.

The airline was reactivated in December 1944 after a lull caused by the war, and within one year commenced flights to London. Initially, the Avro York served this long-range route, later being replaced by the DC-4 and Constellation. In October 1953 two Comet Is were leased from BOAC as fore-runners of a jetliner fleet. Owing to the Comet I accidents, this episode was short-lived.

Introducing the DC-7B in 1954, SAA began Australian services, and in October 1960 it joined in the jet race with Boeing 707s, operated on the European routes. In 1969 the South Atlantic route to Rio de Janeiro by way of New York was opened, and the 747 was first introduced in 1971.

SAA now flies to more than ten nations in Europe, to the USA, Brazil and Argentina in the west, and to Australia, Hong Kong and Taiwan in the east. Within Africa, South Africa's apartheid laws restrict the number of countries to which SAA may fly, and the airline is even obliged to fly to Europe across the Atlantic.

Air Afrique

A joint venture by 11 nations formerly under the French colonies (Cameroon, Central Africa, Congo, Ivory Coast, Benin, Gabon, Upper Volta, Mauritania, Niger, Senegal and Chad), Aer Afrique was formed in March 1961. Later, Togo joined and Cameroon and Gabon withdrew, setting the present number of partners at ten. The airline's formation was suggested by Air France and UAT (now UTA), and a subsidiary of these two companies, Sodetrat, held 34 per cent control (now 28 per cent), and leased the equipment at the outset.

Apart from local networks covering the partner countries, Air Afrique's services extend to Europe and the USA. Its ten-aircraft fleet includes DC-10s, DC-8s, A300s, and one 747-200F.

Air Madagascar

Located east of the African continent, Madagascar had long been under French administration before its independence in 1960.

Air Madagascar began as TIA, formed in 1947 to serve the local network. TIA became Madair in 1960 with the Government holding 20 per cent of the shares, Air France 44 per cent, and Air Madagascar 36 per cent. In October 1961 Madair leased the DC-7C to open its Paris route. Madair was then renamed Air Madagascar, now 80 per cent under Government control.

Primarily serving the island, Air Madagascar's international services are restricted to the adjacent islands, East African countries, Paris and Rome, For long-range routes it has one 747-200B in its fleet, which otherwise comprises one 737 and propeller-driven aircraft.

Air Gabon

A small airstrip located near the Dr
Schweitzer hospital in the midst of
jungles at Lambarene is served occas-
ionally by a small aeroplane which
provides a link with civilisation. This
service was arranged by Transgabon, Air
Gabon's predecessor.

Transgabon was formed in 1951 to
serve local routes and transport air cargo
to remote locations. The present name
was assumed in 1974.

Following its independence from
France in 1961, Gabon joined Air
Afrique. It left the consortium in 1977,
and Air Gabon became an independent
national airline flying international
routes. One 747-200 Combi was purchased to be put on the European
services. For short-range services, 737s
and F-28s are used.

Cameroon Airlines

Like Air Gabon and Air Madagascar,
this airline operates long-range services
with one 747-200 Combi. For local and
neighbouring destinations in Africa it
uses 737s and Twin Otters.

Once a member of Air Afrique,
Cameroon withdrew in 1971 and formed
Cameroon Airlines, with the Government and Air France holding 70 and 30
per cent respectively. Air Cameroon,
which had been operating since 1950,
was absorbed.

Cameroon Airlines commenced operation in November 1971 with piston-
engined DC-4s. These were replaced by
737s, and the airline also purchased one
707 which was replaced by a 747 in 1982.